Great **Rivers** *of the World*

THE AMAZON

THE AMAZON

Edward Parker

WORLD ALMANAC® LIBRARY

Please visit our web site at: www.worldalmanaclibrary.com
For a free color catalog describing World Almanac® Library's list of high-quality books and
multimedia programs, call 1-800-848-2928 (USA) or 1-800-387-3178 (Canada). World Almanac®
Library's fax: (414) 332-3567.

Library of Congress Cataloging-in-Publication Data

Parker, Edward, 1961-
    The Amazon / Edward Parker.
        p. cm. — (Great rivers of the world)
    Includes bibliographical references and index.
    Contents: The course of the river — The Amazon in history — Cities and settlements —
Economic activity — Animals and plants — Environmental issues — Leisure and recreation —
The future.
    ISBN 0-8368-5442-X (lib. bdg.)
    ISBN 0-8368-5449-7 (softcover)
    1. Amazon River—Juvenile literature. [1. Amazon River.] I. Title. II. Series.
  F2546.P274   2003
  981'.1—dc21   2002033114

First published in 2003 by
World Almanac® Library
330 West Olive Street, Suite 100
Milwaukee, WI 53212 USA

Copyright © 2003 by World Almanac® Library.

Developed by Monkey Puzzle Media
Editor: Jane Bingham
Designer: Tim Mayer
Picture researcher: Lynda Lines
World Almanac® Library editor: Jim Mezzanotte
World Almanac® Library art direction: Tammy Gruenewald

Picture acknowledgements
All photos by Edward Parker, except: Corbis, cover (Yann Arthus-Bertrand), 9 (Arvind Garg);
Still Pictures, 4 (Andre Bartschi), 10 top (NASA), 13 (Edward Parker). Map artwork by Peter Bull.

Printed in the United States of America

1 2 3 4 5 6 7 8 9 07 06 05 04 03

CONTENTS

INTRODUCTION

INTRODUCTION

A Giant River

The Amazon is the world's largest river. It flows through the South American continent for 4,007 miles (6,448 kilometers), from its **source** in an icy stream high up in the Andes Mountains to its gigantic **mouth** on the Atlantic coast. Although it is not the longest river in the world — the Nile River in Africa is 127 miles (204 km) longer — it is the largest in terms of the amount of water it discharges into the ocean. The Amazon River has more water flowing in it than the world's next eight largest rivers put together.

AMAZON FACTS

- Length: 4,007 miles (6,448 km)
- Drainage basin: 2.7 million sq miles (7 million sq km)
- Main cities: Manaus (Brazil), Belém (Brazil), Santarém (Brazil), Pôrto Velho (Brazil), Iquitos (Peru), Pucallpa (Peru)
- Delta width: 150–200 miles (240–320 km)

The Amazon River flows for thousands of miles through the world's largest area of rain forest.

An Enormous Basin

The Amazon River is surrounded by a vast river **basin**. This basin contains thousands of streams and rivers, called **tributaries**. The streams join together to form larger and larger rivers, all of which run into the Amazon River. The Amazon basin covers an area almost as large as the continental United States.

The Amazon Rain Forest

Huge areas of the Amazon River basin consist of rain forest. The Amazon rain forest covers more than 750,000 square miles (1,950,000 sq km). The largest remaining rain forest in the world, it contains countless **species** of plants and animals, as well as groups of Native people who live deep within it and have little contact with the outside world.

This rain forest has long been a place of mystery. There are rumors of animals still waiting to be discovered in the Amazon rain forest, as well as legends of ancient golden cities lying deep within its interior regions. Even today, explorers set off down the Amazon River, searching for adventure.

Jaguars are the largest meat-eating mammals in the Amazon rain forest. Unlike most big cats, jaguars are strong swimmers.

Chapter 1

THE COURSE OF THE RIVER
THE COURSE OF THE RIVER

FINDING THE AMAZON

Vincente Pincon was the first European to find the Amazon. In 1500, he captained a Spanish ship that was 120 miles (200 km) off the coast of Brazil when the crew realized they were sailing through fresh water. Pincon followed the fresh water back to the coast, and he discovered the mouth of the Amazon. The mouth of the river was so large that he named it *Mar Dulce*, or "Freshwater Sea."

The Prehistoric Amazon

In geological terms, the Amazon River basin is very old. **Geologists** have discovered that water was flowing through the Amazon basin about 150 million years ago, when dinosaurs were still roaming Earth. The prehistoric Amazon River, however, was very different from the river of today. Millions of years ago, the river actually flowed in the opposite direction than it does now.

This map shows the course of the Amazon River and its main tributaries.

6

An Inland Sea

Originally, the Amazon River flowed west into the Pacific Ocean. About 120 million years ago, however, two of the vast plates that form part of Earth's surface began to push into each other along the western side of South America. As they did so, land was slowly pushed up for thousands of feet. Over millions of years, the Andes Mountains were formed. This high mountain range prevented the Amazon River from reaching the Pacific

Millions of years ago, the Amazon River flowed west. Its course eventually was blocked by the high Andes Mountains (above). Now the river flows east.

Ocean. The water in the river, however, continued to flow west for several million years, resulting in a huge inland sea that was about the size of the Mediterranean Sea today.

The Modern Amazon

This inland sea remained cut off by the Andes Mountains until about 80 million years ago, when the whole continent of South America started tilting downward to the east. The land eventually tilted so much that the waters of the inland sea spilled through a gap between the highlands of present-day Brazil and Guyana and found their way to the Atlantic Ocean. For the past 60 million years, the Amazon River has been flowing from west to east, across the continent of South America.

Today, the Amazon River's water is collected from a basin that covers half of South America and includes parts of the present-day countries of Bolivia, Brazil, Colombia, Ecuador, Guyana, Suriname, Venezuela, and French Guiana.

Source of the Amazon

The Amazon River is formed in Peru by the confluence, or coming together, of the Marañón and Ucayali Rivers. The Ucayali River is fed by the Apurimac River. The source of the Apurimac River is considered to be the Amazon River's source, because compared to other possible sources, it is the farthest distance from the mouth of the Amazon.

Until recently, no one was sure exactly where this source was located. In 2000, however, a team of scientists found what is believed to be the source of the Amazon. It is a small stream that flows high in the Andes Mountains in Peru, less than 100 miles (160 km) from the Pacific coast.

Thousands of small mountain streams in the Andes combine to form tributaries of the Amazon River.

Tributaries

The tributaries of the Amazon consist of thousands of mountain streams and rivers that combine to form larger and larger rivers. Some tributaries start flowing near South America's Pacific coast and run for hundreds of miles before joining the Amazon River. They form a network of waterways that drain the Amazon basin.

Most of the Amazon River's tributaries begin as streams high up in the Andes Mountains, but a number of the major tributaries start in other highland areas. The Trombetas River, for example, begins in the Guyanan Highlands of Venezuela. Other large rivers, such as the Xingu River and the Tapajós River, start as small streams in the central highlands of Brazil.

The tributaries of the Amazon that flow from the Andes Mountains are pale brown in color because of the **silt** they are carrying. Tributaries joining the Amazon from the north, such as the Negro River, are usually black in color. At the Brazilian city of Manaus, the two different-colored waters meet, and the colors run side by side for more than 10 miles (17 km).

Progress of a River

In Peru, the Apurimac River joins the Urubama River to form the Ucayali River. The Ucayali then joins the Marañón River to become the Amazon River. In the western region of Brazil, the Amazon River is also called the Solimoes River. After the Negro River joins the Solimoes, near the city of Manaus, the Solimoes is known as the Amazon River.

TRIBUTARY FACTS

- The Amazon River receives water from over 15,000 tributaries.
- Twelve of the Amazon's tributaries are over 1,000 miles (1,600 km) long.
- The Madiera-Mamoré-Grande River is 2,100 miles (3,380 km) long. It is the world's longest tributary and the 14th largest river in the world.
- During the rainy season, about 1.25 million miles (2 million km) of rivers in the Amazon basin are **navigable** by ship.

Near Manaus, the black waters of the Negro River join the pale brown waters of the Amazon River, and they flow beside each other before mixing together.

The Flooded Forest

Beyond the Andes mountain range, the water of the
Amazon River moves slowly. The wide river **meanders**
across a vast plain. On this central plain, reminders of
the ancient inland sea of prehistoric times can be found.

During the dry season, the Amazon River is more
than a mile wide as it flows past Manaus, in central Brazil.
During the wet season, however, its waters can rise by
as much as 50 feet (15 meters), covering large areas of
rain forest and forming a huge flooded area twice the size
of New Jersey. This area is known as the flooded forest.
More than 1,000 species of fish travel to the flooded
forest each year to lay their eggs. Some, such as
stingrays, are descendants of fish that were
trapped millions of years ago in the inland
sea. The pink freshwater dolphin —
another water creature found in
the flooded forest — is
descended from the
dolphins that swam
in the inland sea.

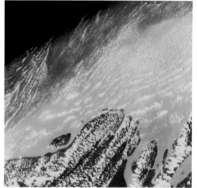

*This aerial view of the Amazon **delta**
shows silt from the Amazon River being
sent out into the Atlantic Ocean.*

> **❝ I live in the village of San Miguel, near Santarém. We live on an island in the middle of the river. Normally we build our houses more than 150 feet [45 m] from the river's edge. This is because the river is so powerful that sometimes large parts of the island are washed away. Sometimes entire islands disappear, and new ones are forming all the time. ❞**
> Antonio Cavalho

The Amazon Delta

A delta is an area where a river empties into the sea through a fan-shaped network of channels. The Amazon delta is the largest river delta in the world. It begins east of where the Xingu River joins the Amazon River, about 155 miles (250 km) from the Atlantic Ocean. Here, the river splits into a maze of channels and islands. One of these islands, Marajó, is larger than the state of Massachusetts.

The Amazon River does not stop flowing when it reaches the ocean. The river's flow of water as it enters the ocean is estimated to average 55 million gallons (210 million liters) a second. Water from the Amazon River continues to flow more than 150 miles (240 km) out to sea.

This photograph shows part of the flooded forest in the dry season. During the rainy season, the trees are almost entirely covered by water.

Chapter 2

THE AMAZON IN HISTORY
THE AMAZON IN HISTORY

Early Peoples of the Amazon

TRAVELING THE AMAZON

In 1542, the Spanish explorer Francisco de Orellana became the first European to travel the Amazon River. Attracted by rumors of a city built of gold deep inside the rain forest, Orellana and his men set out on an incredible journey from Peru to the Atlantic coast. Like many Europeans who explored South America, Orellana hoped to become fabulously rich.

Scholars have long thought that the first people to live in the Amazon basin were Stone Age hunters who probably came from Asia. Some evidence suggests that people crossed from northern Asia to North America on a large mass of land about 15,000 to 20,000 years ago and spread out through North America and then into South America, arriving in the Amazon basin around 8,000 years ago.

Most signs of early people, such as skeletal remains, disappeared long ago because the Amazon basin's humid climate caused them to disintegrate. Some **fossils** of animal bones, however, have been discovered in the basin. These fossils indicate that early humans hunted wild animals such as deer and tapir (small, piglike animals). They may even have hunted a giant animal, called a sloth, that measured up to 15 feet (4.5 m) tall and weighed up to 5 tons (4.5 metric tons)!

Archaeologists have discovered pieces of pottery and stone ax heads near Manaus. This evidence indicates that a large number of **Amerindians** lived in the central Amazon basin 5,000 years ago. Closer to the Atlantic coast, on the island of Marajó, archaeologists have discovered beautifully decorated pots and piles of sea shells dating from the same period. These artifacts suggest that early people were living settled and sophisticated lives in the Amazon delta.

This pot is a copy of one made in the Amazon delta about 3,000 years ago.

An Earlier People?

Some experts are now challenging the idea that all the people of the Amazon basin originally came from Asia. They think that there may have been earlier civilizations established by humans from Africa or from the Polynesian islands. New evidence suggests that some people may have settled in the Amazon basin more than 12,000 years ago.

European Settlement

The first Europeans reached South America in the 1490s. By the middle of the 1500s, thousands of European settlers had arrived. Most early settlers were Spanish or Portuguese, but later settlers came from other European countries, such as Britain and Germany.

Spanish and Portuguese settlers had hoped to make their fortunes by finding gold. Instead, most of them grew sugar and tobacco on large farms called plantations. The Europeans used local Native people as slaves on their plantations and forced them to work incredibly hard. Millions of the Amazon basin's Native

Like many people in the Amazon region, this family is descended from both Amerindians and Europeans.

*The mountain city of Machu Picchu, located in present-day Peru, was built by a Native people known as the **Inca** just before Europeans arrived in South America.*

people died from overwork and from European diseases such as measles and influenza.

The arrival of the Europeans had a disastrous impact on the Native people. It is impossible to determine the exact number of people living in the Amazon basin when the Europeans arrived, but it is thought to have been more than seven million. Within a century, this number had shrunk to less than a million.

Since traveling through the Amazon rain forest was so difficult, most European settlements and farms were built along the banks of rivers. Few Europeans ventured away from the riverbanks, aside from prospectors searching for gold and missionaries seeking Native people to convert to Christianity.

Wealth from Rubber

In the mid-1800s, the Amazon basin briefly fulfilled its promise of fabulous riches for the European settlers. This wealth came from an unlikely source — a white, sticky substance called latex that oozed out of the bark of certain trees. The latex could be turned into rubber, which was used to make waterproof clothing, tires, and other products. By the late 1800s, factories around the world needed rubber in huge quantities. The "rubber boom" lasted from 1870 to 1920 and created vast fortunes for the so-called rubber barons. The cities of Manaus, Belém, and Iquitos, all on the banks of the Amazon River, became major ports for exporting rubber to the rest of the world.

The elegant Teatro de Paz in Belém, Brazil, was built at the height of the rubber boom.

Although many Europeans made their fortunes from rubber, the rubber boom took a huge toll on the Native people of the Amazon basin. Thousands of Native people were forced to gather the latex and process it into rubber. Scholars have calculated that for every ton of rubber produced, seven people died.

A Deadly Rubber Boom

In 1912, a British newspaper, *The Illustrated London News*, reported that the Peruvian Amazon Rubber Company had been responsible for the deaths of more than 30,000 Witoto Indians in the area of the Amazon basin where it collected rubber. Five years later, an inquiry revealed that the true number of Indians that died as a result of the company's activities was 42,000.

The Amazon Basin in the Twentieth Century

By the 1920s, the rubber boom had collapsed. The British had managed to smuggle some rubber tree seedlings out of the Amazon basin, and they were soon producing rubber more cheaply in Southeast Asia. In the space of a few years, many people in the Amazon basin lost their fortunes.

Gold, extracted from mines such as this one, is just one of many valuable metals that lie beneath the Amazon rain forest.

IRON WEALTH

Brazil is estimated to have approximately 48 billion tons (43.5 billion m tons) of iron ore waiting to be mined, and almost all of this iron is in the Amazon basin region. At the current rate of mining, this iron should last for the next 500 years.

Over the next forty years, as two world wars raged, the Amazon region was largely forgotten by the rest of the world. After World War II, however, some South American countries saw an opportunity to make money from the Amazon region. With the help of U.S. and European banks, Brazil and other countries began making plans to take advantage of the Amazon basin's natural resources, such as timber and iron ore. Roads were built, dams were constructed to produce electricity, and tens of thousands of workers flooded into the Amazon basin to find jobs on new farming and construction projects.

PROBLEM PROJECT

During the 1980s, the World Bank helped Brazil develop a large part of the Amazon rain forest through an ambitious plan called the Polonoreste Project. Between 1981 and 1985, Brazil created new farming areas, built roads, and provided isolated areas with services such as electricity, hospitals, and schools. Instead of providing controlled development, however, the Polonoreste Project led to enormous problems. Huge numbers of of new workers cut down large areas of precious forest and invaded the lands of the region's Native people.

The Amazon region has large reserves of oil and gas. This pipeline in Ecuador takes oil over the Andes Mountains to oil refineries on the Pacific coast.

New Riches

Toward the end of the twentieth century, huge reserves of oil and the **minerals** iron ore and gold were discovered beneath the Amazon rain forest, leading to the establishment of oil wells and mines. More than a million gold miners — known as *garimperos* — arrived in the Amazon basin. Today, mining, fishing, logging, agriculture, and cattle ranching are important activities in the Amazon basin, and workers still pour into the region in search of jobs and a better life.

Chapter 3

CITIES AND SETTLEMENTS

CITIES AND SETTLEMENTS

The famous Manaus Opera House was built in 1896. It now stands at the heart of a large, modern city.

Manaus (Brazil)

Manaus is the largest city in the Amazon basin, with a population of more than 1.25 million. It stands at the meeting point of the Amazon and the Negro Rivers, almost exactly in the middle of the Amazon basin. Despite being 900 miles (1,450 km) upstream from the Atlantic Ocean, it is a thriving international port, with docks for large, oceangoing vessels.

For almost 400 years, Manaus was a small country town, but the rubber boom led to a drastic change in its development. In the space of thirty years, from 1870 to 1920, Manaus went from a tiny **trading post** to the wealthiest city in South America. Extravagant buildings, such as the Manaus Opera House, were built using the most expensive materials from Europe. By the 1920s, however, the rubber boom had collapsed and the city had lost most of its wealth.

Today, Manaus is a thriving city once again, thanks mostly to its special status in Brazil as a free trade zone, which allows companies to establish businesses in the city without paying taxes. This situation has encouraged many electronics firms to build factories in Manaus and has created many new jobs. The city also has increasing numbers of people employed by banks, restaurants, hotels, and other businesses in the **service industry**.

While Manaus is a modern city in many ways, tens of thousands of people in the city are still employed in such traditional industries as fishing and gathering and packing Brazil nuts.

This map shows the main cities and towns of the Amazon basin.

Belém (Brazil)

After Manaus, Belém is the only other city in the Amazon basin that has a population of more than a million people. Located on the southern side of the Amazon delta, it is mainly an international port. Belém exports huge quantities of Brazil nuts, timber, and other Amazonian products to the rest of the world.

Belém's wealth was orginally based on rubber exports, and, like Manaus, it has some magnificent buildings from the rubber boom era in its old center. The people of Belém, however, are different from those of Manaus. The city's Native people come from different tribes, and many of its inhabitants are descended from Native people and African slaves who were brought to work on plantations near the city in the 1800s. Although Belém has many shopping centers and riverside restaurants in its downtown area, the city is still surrounded by shoddy wooden houses where many of its poorest people live.

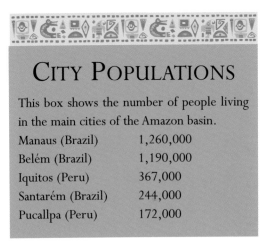

CITY POPULATIONS

This box shows the number of people living in the main cities of the Amazon basin.

Manaus (Brazil)	1,260,000
Belém (Brazil)	1,190,000
Iquitos (Peru)	367,000
Santarém (Brazil)	244,000
Pucallpa (Peru)	172,000

19

Iquitos (Peru)

The most important city in the upper Amazon region is Iquitos in Peru. The city is 2,300 miles (3,700 km) from the Atlantic Ocean and is the furthest port from the ocean that can be reached by oceangoing ships. Like Belém and Manaus, it developed rapidly during the rubber boom. Today, it has a population of more than 350,000, but it still remains largely isolated from the rest of Peru. The only way to reach the city is by boat or plane.

The modern **economy** of Iquitos is based on tourism and oil. Like most cities in the Amazon basin, Iquitos has a central zone with a mixture of old and new buildings and areas of much poorer housing around this center. Many of the houses on the outskirts of Iquitos are built on stilts because of the seasonal flooding on this stretch of the Amazon River.

Santarém (Brazil)

Santarém is one of the fastest-growing and most important cities on the Amazon River. It is a large fishing port that lies about halfway between Manaus and Belém. Santarém is growing rapidly because farmers are cutting down the nearby rain forest to grow crops they can export. In addition, work has begun on a road that will be over 1,200 miles (1,900 km) long, which will link Santarém to the

The city streets of Iquitos, Peru, are busy with cars and motorcycle taxis.

major agricultural areas of central Brazil. The new road and farmland will greatly increase the volume of exports passing through the city over the next twenty years.

> **❝ I am Julio Barboso, and I am the mayor of the town of Xapuri in Brazil. The town has a population of around 10,000 people, and most of the jobs are related to gathering rubber and Brazil nuts. It is not a large town, but we have street lights, and tourists are beginning to come. ❞**

Many Amazonian people live in poorly constructed housing, like these shacks, on the edges of cities.

Towns in the Amazon Basin

Numerous towns are scattered along the Amazon River and its tributaries. Many of these towns were originally trading posts built by Portuguese and Spanish settlers in the sixteenth and seventeenth centuries. Tefé, Brazil, for example, was once famous for its trade in turtle eggs. Today, Tefé is a major center for fishing and logging.

The main routes of communication in the Amazon basin are the region's rivers, and most of its towns are built on high land at the meeting point of two rivers. Rivers in the Amazon basin are still important trading routes, and many towns along them are enjoying a new economic boom. Lago Nueva Lojo Agrio, for example, on the banks of the Aguarico River in Ecuador, is a thriving oil town, while Pucallpa, on the Ucayali River in Peru, is an important producer of oil and timber

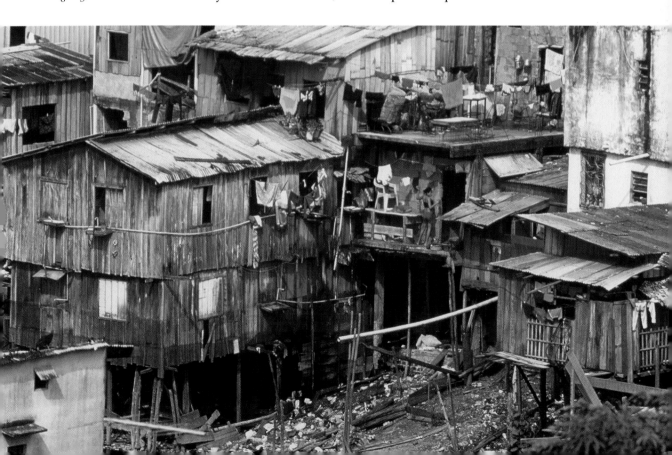

Native Villages

Villages belonging to different groups of Native people are scattered throughout the Amazon basin. High in the Andes Mountains, along the tributaries of the Amazon, descendants of the Inca live in small settlements. In the lowland rain forest, groups such as the Yagua in Colombia, the Mojeno in Bolivia, and the Kayapo in Brazil live in small villages. The Yanomami people of Brazil and Venezuela live in large communal houses, called *mallocas*. These houses can hold up to 200 people.

Many Native villages are built beside rivers. This settlement is on the banks of the Alto Jurua River, a tributary of the Amazon River in Brazil.

CABOCLOS

The *caboclos* live in the Brazilian rain forest. They are the descendants of Native people and Europeans who settled in the Amazon basin more than a hundred years ago. Unlike modern settlers, the caboclos live in a way that is similar to the Amazon basin's Native people — they hunt, fish, and gather fruit, and they cause little damage to their environment.

This area of rain forest has been cut down by migrant settlers to make room for a new house and farm.

Native people living in the Amazon basin cut small plots of land out of the rain forest where they grow **manioc**, bananas, and beans. They usually abandon their villages every few years and move somewhere new to keep from exhausting the soil in their rain forest gardens. They are also expert hunters and fishermen.

Migrant Settlements

Over the past thirty years, tens of thousands of people — almost all of them non-Native — have migrated into the Amazon rain forest. These poor **migrants** have arrived from the surrounding areas in search of land to farm. Most of the migrants, however, have no experience growing food in the rain forest. They usually build a wooden house and cut down the rain forest all around the house to create a small farm. Unlike the Native people, the migrants do not move every few years to allow the forest to recover.

23

Chapter 4

ECONOMIC ACTIVITY

ECONOMIC ACTIVITY

A Range of Industries

For centuries, people have taken advantage of the Amazon basin's natural resources. The region's traditional industries are mining, fishing, logging, and gathering Brazil nuts, and these industries continue to employ large numbers of people. As the region has developed, however, other businesses have become important, especially businesses in the service industry such as tourism and banking. Some parts of the region have seen the growth of modern industries, such as Japanese electronic companies in Manaus.

Workers near a sawmill in Pucallpa, Peru, attach a rope to a rain forest log so it can be hauled out of the water.

Logging

Considering that the Amazon basin has the largest area of rain forest in the world, it is not surprising that the timber industry plays an important role in the local economy. Tens of thousands of people are involved in cutting down and processing timber. Loggers cut down trees deep in the rain forest, then use the many rivers to float their logs out of the forest. The logs are cut into lumber in large sawmills in towns and cities such as Iquitos and Manaus. Oceangoing ships then pick up the lumber and export it to other parts of the world.

Fishermen unload their catch at the harbor in Belém. The catch often includes giant piraracus, which live in the Amazon River.

Fishing

Fishing is one of the main economic activities in the Amazon region. More than 2,000 species of fish live in the Amazon basin, and many of them sell for high prices. Piranhas, large catfish, and giant pirarucus are all caught along the Amazon River. Large quantities of fish are eaten by the people who live in the growing towns and cities of the Amazon basin, but thousands of tons of fish are also exported to be made into animal food.

Some people in the Amazon basin still catch fish in the traditional way, from wooden canoes using spears and small nets. Others work on large **trawlers**, equipped with freezers, that can stay out of port for weeks at a time. In addition to the people involved in fishing, tens of thousands of people work transporting the fish and selling it in bustling markets throughout the Amazon region.

> **❝** *My name is Jorge Cavalho, and I work in the fish market in Belém. Belém is an important fishing center because it is close enough to the ocean for the market to sell fish from the ocean and from the Amazon River. Hundreds of us work in the market, and we sell everything from sharks to piranhas.* **❞**

FARMING FIGURES

The state of Para, Brazil, is almost twice as large as Texas and has a population of more than 5 million. In 1999, its farmers produced these crops:

- 3,748,878 tons (3,400,982 m tons) of manioc
- 386,878 tons (350,976 m tons) of rice
- 629,613 tons (571,185 m tons) of corn
- 231,659,000 pineapples
- 143,402,000 coconuts

Agriculture

Large areas of the Amazon rain forest have been cleared for use as farmland. Farmers grow crops such as oil palm, **soya**, sugar cane, bananas, beans, and manioc, and they export most of their produce to other countries. In Ecuador, large areas of forest have been replaced by oil palm plantations. In Brazil, Bolivia, and Venezuela, parts of the rain forest have been converted into ranches for cattle. Most of the beef from Amazonian cattle is eaten in the countries where the cattle are raised, but large quantities of this beef are also used for hamburger meat as far away as the United States.

Recently, farmers have begun to grow large amounts of soya, which is used in animal feed and is an ingredient in many processed foods. Soya is a valuable crop that earns important foreign income.

Mining

An incredible wealth of minerals and oil lies under the ground in the Amazon basin. Some of the world's largest deposits of gold, bauxite (a form of aluminum), iron ore, and oil have been discovered in the region. In Brazil and Venezuela, more than a million gold miners pan for gold in the Amazon River. In Ecuador and Peru, vast reserves of oil are pumped out of the ground, while the Grande Carajas project in Brazil is a major center for mining iron ore.

FINDING IRON

In 1968, a survey helicopter developed engine trouble and made an emergency landing on a hill in the Carajas mountain range in Brazil. While the helicopter was being repaired, one of the geologists on board discovered that almost the entire hill consisted of high-grade iron ore. Today, the Carajas mine is the largest iron ore mine in the world.

At the market at Pizac, near Cuzco in Peru, farmers sell a variety of fruits and vegetables.

Service Industry

The fastest growing segment of the Amazon basin's economy is the service industry, which includes banks, hotels, restaurants, and tourist agencies. As towns and cities have expanded, the need for all the services found in modern cities has increased. Large numbers of people in the Amazon region now work in offices.

The Shipibo Indians in Peru are famous for their pottery. Many Shipibo Indians now sell pots to tourists.

Sustainable Activities

Two of the major industries in the Amazon basin, mining and logging, have caused serious environmental problems in the region. Mining causes pollution, for example, while logging clears large areas of rain forest. Farming has also involved clearing huge stretches of forest. In contrast to this wasteful destruction are the traditional activities still practiced by many people in the Amazon region, activities that cause little damage to the environment.

Tens of thousands of people, for example, gather latex and Brazil nuts from wild trees in the rain forest and do not chop the trees down to create large plantations. Some fruits that grow wild in the forest, such as the acai palm fruit, are harvested by local people.

Some logging companies are developing new logging methods that do not involve cutting down large areas of forest. The loggers take only a few trees in each square mile of forest and leave the other trees standing. Companies are also ending the practice of cutting down and burning any trees that are not worth turning into lumber.

All these activities, in which people try to work within their natural environment instead of destroying it, are known as sustainable activities. These activities can have a big impact on the tourist industry. Today, many people will pay large amounts of money to go on tours where they can see wild animals living in undisturbed areas of forest.

WILD RUBBER GATHERERS

Over 500,000 people in the Amazon rain forest earn most of their income gathering latex from wild rubber trees. This activity causes very little damage to the forest.

Chapter 5

ANIMALS AND PLANTS

Mammals

A wide variety of mammals live in the Amazon basin. River animals like the giant otter and the capybara live on the riverbanks, and dolphins swim in the rivers. Most mammals in the Amazon basin, however, stay hidden deep inside the rain forest.

The rain forest is made up of many layers, from the thick vegetation covering the forest floor to the tops of trees, known as the forest **canopy**. Over 200 species of mammals (not including bats) live in the Amazon rain forest. Each species has its special place, or niche, in the forest.

Tapirs and brocket deer live on the forest floor, where they eat leaves and fallen fruit. Small monkeys, such as the pygmy marmoset, and tree anteaters live in the lower levels of the forest and are often found along the edges of rivers. Higher in the trees, sloths and monkeys such as the white uakari feed on leaves, fruit, and nuts. Even higher, in the rain forest canopy, woolly monkeys and howler monkeys can sometimes be glimpsed as they scamper through the highest branches looking for fruit and leaves.

The uakari monkey has a scarlet face and long, shaggy white fur. Found only in a small area of the Amazon basin, it is very rare.

JAGUARS

The jaguar is the Amazon basin's most fearsome hunter. It can grow up to 8 feet (2.5 m) long and weigh as much as 300 pounds (135 kilograms). It is an excellent climber and eats many kinds of birds and animals, but its favorite prey is the peccary (a small pig). Unlike most cats, it is a strong swimmer and catches fish and caiman (a kind of alligator).

The rain forest is also home to some fierce hunters — the jaguar, the puma, and the ocelot. These wild cats are carnivores (meat-eaters) that prey on smaller mammals and birds.

Birds

Birds are one of the most visible groups of animals in the rain forest. Large flocks of water birds, such as ducks and egrets, live on rivers and lakes, and parrots and toucans squawk and chatter loudly as they fly around the forest in large, noisy groups.

Other species of birds in the rain forest are much harder to spot. Tiny hummingbirds dart between flowers to feed on nectar, while black-fronted nunbirds sit patiently on branches waiting to catch juicy insects that fly past.

The Amazon rain forest is also home to the harpy eagle — a giant hawk that feeds on sloths and monkeys. Altogether, at least 1,750 species of birds live in the Amazon basin.

This chestnut-fronted parrot is one of many colorful parrots that live in the Amazon rain forest. Parrots gather in noisy flocks to feed on seeds and fruits high in the trees.

Insects and Spiders

So many different kinds of insects and spiders live in the Amazon rain forest that scientists can only guess at their numbers. It is estimated, however, that 90 percent of the world's insects live in tropical rain forests in various parts of the world. Beautiful morpho butterflies with brilliant, metallic blue wings; giant bird-eating spiders; and delicate damselflies with silvery bodies and long, transparent wings all live in the Amazon rain forest.

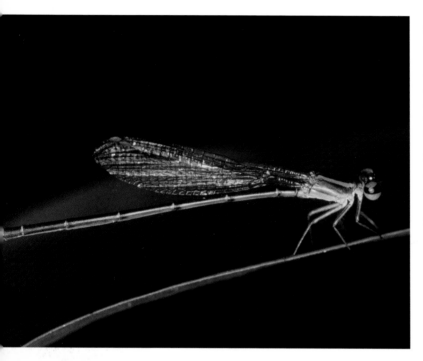

A delicate Amazonian damselfly rests on a plant stem. These insects catch and eat other small flying insects.

Reptiles

The Amazon rain forest is home to some of the world's most spectacular reptiles, including large snakes such as the green anaconda (considered the world's largest snake) and the boa constrictor, as well as the black caiman, a kind of alligator that can weigh more than a ton. Various turtles live in the rivers of the Amazon basin, including the large Amazonian river turtle and the matmata, which is a turtle that spends most of its time underwater with just its tubular nose poking above the surface. The Amazon basin is also home to many poisonous snakes, including the bushmaster, the coral snake, and the eyelash viper.

AMAZING FINDS

In the 1800s, an English naturalist, Henry Walter Bates, spent eleven years in the Amazon rain forest. He brought back 14,712 insect specimens. Eight thousand of these specimens were new to science.

Amphibians

Amphibians can live on land, but they lay their eggs in water, and most of them need to stay moist and warm to survive. The Amazon rain forest provides a perfect **habitat** for amphibians, and many species thrive there. The most common kinds of amphibians are frogs and toads. They come in a spectacular range of colors and sizes, from the brightly colored poison arrow frog, which is about the size of a man's thumbnail, to the cane toad, which can grow to be over 8 inches (20 cm) long. The cecaellian lives in the rain forest, but it is rarely seen. It is a legless amphibian that burrows through the soil looking for insects to eat.

Turtles are often found in and around the Amazon River. These turtles are warming themselves in the sun before diving into the river to look for food.

This brilliantly colored plant is a heliconia. The nectar inside its flowers can only be reached by tiny, long-billed hummingbirds.

Plants

When early European explorers first entered the Amazon rain forest, they were amazed by the variety of trees and other plants they found. The soil in the Amazon rain forest is very thin, but many trees in the forest grow more than 130 feet (40 m) high. Many rain forest trees have buttress roots. These roots grow out from a tree's trunk above the ground and provide extra support for the tree, which has underground roots that are very shallow. Trees in the rain forest are often covered by plants known as **epiphytes**. An epiphyte is a plant that grows on another plant without causing it harm. Epiphytes include mosses, ferns, orchids, and bromeliads (plants with cuplike leaves for catching water).

In the Amazon rain forest, dense tangles of vegetation often form, with long vines hanging down from enormous trees. A plant known as the strangler fig coils around a large tree as it grows. The strangler fig eventually crushes the tree.

Many of the trees and other plants in the Amazon rain forest produce spectacular flowers. The heliconia plant, for example, has bright yellow, orange, and red flowers. The rain forest is also home to more than 100 species of flowering orchids. Many of these orchids have brilliantly colored petals.

THE GIANT AMAZON WATER LILY

The giant Amazon water lily has large, round leaves that measure up to 7 feet (2 m) across. The plant grows new leaves every year, and the new leaves grow as much as an inch (2.5 cm) a day.

Fish

More than 2,000 species of fish are estimated to swim in the rivers, streams, and lakes of the Amazon basin. These fish include piranhas, catfish, and the world's second largest freshwater fish, the pirarucu, which can weigh more than 500 pounds (225 kg). Perhaps the most famous fish in the Amazon basin is the piranha. Some kinds of piranhas are extremely aggressive and have a reputation for being able to strip the flesh from an animal the size of a cow in minutes. The millions of fish in the Amazon basin provide food for humans and also for river animals such as the pink dolphin and giant otter.

This fisherman in the flooded forest in Brazil has just caught a catfish.

Chapter 6

ENVIRONMENTAL ISSUES

ENVIRONMENTAL ISSUES

Destroying the Rain Forest

Today, the Amazon region faces many problems. The most serious problem is the destruction of the rain forest through mining, logging, road building, and clearing land for farming and ranching.

This **deforestation** has serious consequences for both the Amazon basin and the region's rivers. When an area of rain forest is destroyed, the habitat for thousands of animal and plant species is also destroyed. In addition, once the forest has been removed, rain washes away the topsoil, making it difficult for the forest to recover. The soil is washed into rivers and streams, which often become silted up and even blocked, changing the flow of the river and affecting the way fish behave.

Clearing rain forest from a large area also results in less rain falling in that area. The rain forest acts like a vast sponge, absorbing rainwater and then slowly releasing the water back into the atmosphere in the form of water vapor. The water vapor forms rain clouds and more rain falls. When an area of the rain forest is destroyed, however, rainwater runs quickly over the bare earth, so very little water **evaporates** into the atmosphere and less rain falls. This problem is becoming worse each year.

VANISHING RAIN FOREST

Ten years ago, the Amazon rain forest was approximately 190,000 square miles (490,000 sq km) bigger than it is now.

About 6,500 square miles (16,800 sq km) of Amazon rain forest is destroyed every year, and this figure is rising.

Large areas of rain forest have been burned to provide grazing lands for cattle. This photograph shows cattle grazing on recently cleared land.

Creating Farmland

In many parts of the Amazon basin, large areas of rain forest have been converted into farmland so that people can grow crops and raise cattle. Around Nueva Loja, in Ecuador, vast plantations have been established for growing coffee beans and oil palms. In Brazil, there are plans to expand the areas of land used for growing soya beans. The rain forest is often cleared in a wasteful and destructive way — trees are bulldozed and then burned where they fall, instead of being taken away and used.

An area of rain forest near Santarém is being burned so that soya beans can be grown.

Mines, Dams, and Roads

Large-scale economic projects in the Amazon basin have led to the destruction of the rain forest. Massive mines have been dug under the forest, and dams have been built on the region's rivers. These dams, which are used to produce **hydroelectricity**, have caused widespread flooding in the forests. In addition, an increasing network of roads through the Amazon basin is helping landless migrants enter untouched areas of rain forest. The migrants clear new areas of forest to create their farms, adding to the deforestation.

Pollution

Pollution is a serious problem for the Amazon River and its tributaries. Oil from mines in Ecuador has frequently spilled into the Amazon River, and the growing towns and cities along its banks are producing much more waste and sewage than ever before. The most dangerous pollution of all, however, is caused by gold miners who flush poisonous mercury into the Amazon River and its tributaries. This mercury is having a devastating effect on the fish and plants in the region's rivers and streams and is also poisoning the animals and people that drink from these waters.

A hyacinth macaw is perched beside its nesting place in an old tree. As trees like this one are cut down, the macaws are dying out.

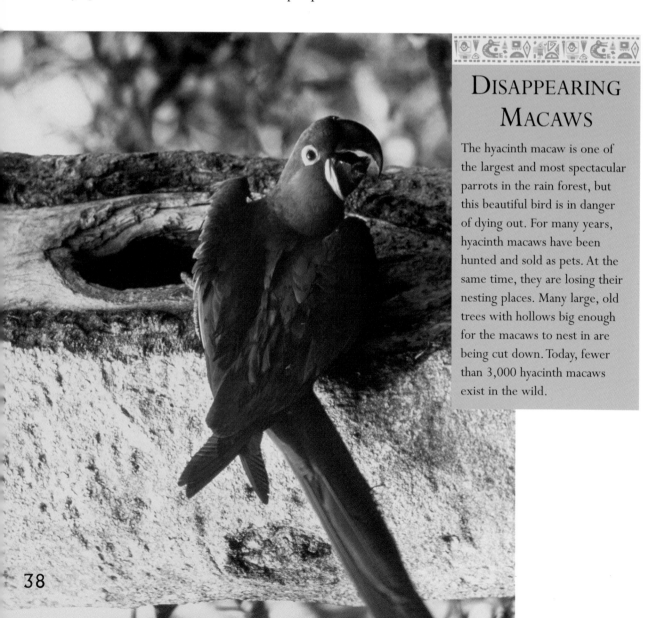

DISAPPEARING MACAWS

The hyacinth macaw is one of the largest and most spectacular parrots in the rain forest, but this beautiful bird is in danger of dying out. For many years, hyacinth macaws have been hunted and sold as pets. At the same time, they are losing their nesting places. Many large, old trees with hollows big enough for the macaws to nest in are being cut down. Today, fewer than 3,000 hyacinth macaws exist in the wild.

Hunting and Fishing

Many creatures in the Amazon basin are under threat from fishing and hunting. Fleets of large fishing trawlers have been taking so many fish from the region's rivers that the numbers of some fish species have been falling dramatically and their stocks have been drastically reduced.

The hunting of animals is also widespread. People living in remote rain forest communities rely on catching land animals, birds, and fish to add to their diet of vegetables, nuts, and fruit. Thousands of people hunt animals such as monkeys and parrots to sell as pets in South America and abroad. A major international market exists for the skins of rare animals, such as jaguars, ocelots, and black caimans, that live in the Amazon rain forest. In addition, the eggs of rare Amazonian turtles are served in expensive restaurants in South American cities such as São Paulo, Brazil.

This fisherman has just caught a caiman. In the Amazon basin, caimans are often hunted for their valuable skins.

Conservation in the Amazon Rain Forest

Many individuals and organizations are fighting hard to slow down the destruction of the rain forest. They are also trying to find ways to save the amazing wildlife in and around the Amazon River. These people have put pressure on governments and large companies that have helped destroy the rain forest in the past. In response to this pressure, some governments and companies are developing practices to avoid destroying the precious environment of the Amazon basin.

These people near Santarém are taking part in a project to release young turtles into the river. The turtles are cared for until they are large enough to survive on their own. Projects such as this one are helping to increase the numbers of turtles in the Amazon basin.

INHERITORS OF THE PLANET

In Colombia, high in the Andes Mountains at the very edge of the Amazon basin, there is an organization called Inheritors of the Planet. These children campaign to save the rain forest near their homes. One of their campaigns was so successful that the president of Colombia made *Laguna de la Cocha* ("Cocha Lake"), where nearly 200 of the children live, a protected area, saving it from a proposed hydroelectric dam project.

Local Protests

Throughout the Amazon basin, brave local people have protested the destruction of the rain forest and the pollution of the Amazon River and its tributaries, even if doing so has put their lives in danger. In 1988, for example, Chico Mendes, a rubber tapper in Brazil, was killed while trying to stop more rain forest from being converted into cattle ranches. Since then, his fellow rubber tappers have successfully established reserves, which are areas where the forest is protected. They have also set up farming cooperatives so that all the people working to gather Brazil nuts and latex for rubber can have a share in the money that is earned.

Groups of Native people in the Amazon basin have been fighting to keep their traditional lands, which would otherwise be destroyed by loggers, cattle ranchers, and migrant farmers. Communities have joined together to protect important lakes where fish breed, and to stop commercial trawlers from over-fishing.

Environmental Organizations

Many environmental organizations, such as the World Wildlife Fund (WWF) and Friends of the Earth, are campaigning to make sure that some areas of the Amazon rain forest are left untouched and that other areas are managed better. After much campaigning by environmental pressure groups, some logging companies are now using new methods that do not involve cutting down huge areas of forest. Environmental groups have also managed to persuade the governments of some countries, such as Peru and Colombia, to create reserves where Native people and rare rain forest wildlife are protected.

41

Chapter 7

LEISURE AND RECREATION

LEISURE AND RECREATION

Children enjoy a Sunday afternoon in a park located in the center of Belém, Brazil.

Cities and Towns

The larger cities and towns along the Amazon River have many modern **amenities**. In Manaus and Belém, for example, people can shop in large shopping malls, meet friends in cafés, and see the latest movies. In Manaus, people can also visit museums, see an opera, or go to a rock concert. In recent years, Internet cafés and electronic game halls have opened in most of the large cities and towns along the Amazon River, so that people can have access to the Internet and play the latest computer games.

One common feature of life in many cities and towns in the Amazon basin is meeting friends and family in parks. These meetings often involve playing games such as soccer. Near the cities of Manaus, Belém, and Santarém, the Amazon River has golden, sandy beaches along its banks that are popular with sunbathers on weekends. Watching professional sports such as basketball and soccer is also a popular pastime in cities and towns.

People celebrate festivals in towns and villages all along the Amazon River. Most of these festivals are held on important days in the calendar of the Roman Catholic Church. On Easter and on some saints' days, for example, there are colorful processions in the streets. The most popular festival is called Carnival. During Carnival, in February or March, people dress up in costumes, and they party and dance for a whole week.

Small Settlements

In small settlements throughout the Amazon region, children and adults often enjoy swimming in the river and playing soccer. Many children play fishing and hunting games, which help them learn techniques that will be useful later in life.

One of the latest developments in small Amazon communities is the arrival of satellite television. With this technology, even people in the most remote parts of the Amazon basin can watch sports and the latest movies.

Wrestling and pottery-making are popular activities in many traditional Native villages of the Amazon River basin. In the daily lives of most traditional Native people, however, there is no clear distinction between work and leisure time.

Soccer is the one of the most popular pastimes in the Amazon region. Here, people play near the docks in Manaus, Brazil.

Chapter 8
THE FUTURE
THE FUTURE

A Changing River

Each year, the Amazon River changes its course slightly. This change in course is the result of silt that the river and its tributaries pick up high in the Andes Mountains. The silt is dumped in the flat land of the Amazon River's flood plain, causing new islands to build up gradually and new channels to form. Around Santarém, maps of the Amazon River are out of date in less than five years, as islands are swept away during floods and new ones are created farther downstream.

The course of the Amazon River could change dramatically in the future, depending on what happens to the climate in the Amazon basin and the rest of the world. Some areas of the Amazon basin have already experienced less rainfall as a combined result of deforestation and **global warming**. Some scientists fear that changes in the world's climate could lead to the Amazon basin becoming drier in the twenty-first century. At the same time, a rise in the sea level caused by global warming could result in dramatic changes around the mouth of the Amazon.

> **" The rainforests are indeed in danger, but their loss is not inevitable....All our knowledge...must be used to produce programs that will reconcile the needs of the people who live in the forests...with those of industrialists and politicians living around their margins, and those of the people in the world at large who, taking a more distant and long-term view, have realized that the tropical rainforests contain some of the world's greatest treasures. "**
>
> David Attenborough, *The Last Rainforests* (1990)

The future of the Amazon rain forest depends on finding the right balance between the needs of people and the needs of wildlife. Cattle ranching on too large a scale leads to the destruction of the forest and can cause some species to die out.

The Future of the Rain Forest

The magnificent Amazon rain forest is now at risk. Since the beginning of the twentieth century, vast areas of the Amazon rain forest have been destroyed and huge numbers of people have moved into the region. The construction of roads, plantations, mines, pipelines, and hydroelectric dams have all led to the destruction of the rain forest. If this trend continues, the future for the Amazon rain forest and its wildlife is bleak.

The future for the Native people of the rain forest is also uncertain. Native people in the Amazon basin are losing their homes as the rain forest is destroyed, and they are also in danger from such diseases as influenza, measles, chicken pox, and malaria.

This map shows the many islands and waterways in the Amazon delta. Some areas are permanently covered by swamps.

Hope for the Future?

The Amazon basin's Native people, rubber tappers, and Brazil nut gatherers have been working together to save the rain forest and to protect traditional ways of life. Along with environmental organizations, they are trying to stop large projects and to teach settlers how to use the rain forest in a responsible way. If their voices are heard, there will be hope for the Amazon basin.

GLOSSARY

GLOSSARY

amenities: places or things that provide convenience or enjoyment to people.

Amerindians: the first people known to live in North and South America, as well as their present-day descendants.

archaeologists: scientists who study human history by examining the physical remains of past human activity.

basin: the area that is drained by a river and its tributaries.

canopy: the upper layer of a rain forest, which is formed by the tops of trees.

deforestation: the process of clearing a forest by cutting down all of its trees.

delta: a flat, triangular area of land at the mouth of a river.

economy: the way a country or region manages the production and consumption of its goods and services.

epiphytes: plants that do not root in soil and so typically use other plants for support.

evaporate: turn into a gas form.

fossils: remains of plants or animals that have been trapped and preserved in rock.

geologists: scientists who study Earth's structure and development by examining rock and soil.

global warming: a process in which certain gases in the atmosphere absorb more heat, raising the temperatures of Earth's climates.

habitat: the place where a plant or animal lives and grows.

hydroelectricity: electricity created by the power of rushing water.

Inca: Native people who controlled a large empire in South America until the arrival of Spanish explorers in the 1500s.

manioc: a starchy root vegetable.

meanders: takes a winding course.

migrant: a person who moves from one area or country to another.

minerals: substances found in the earth that are not plant or animal material and are obtained by mining.

mouth: the place where a river empties into a larger body of water, such as an ocean.

navigable: able to allow the passage of ships.

service industry: businesses such as banks, hotels, and restaurants that provide services to people.

silt: small particles of dirt found in a river.

source: the point of origin for the waters of a river or stream.

soya: a kind of bean used in many processed foods and in animal food.

species: a kind of animal or plant.

trading post: a site in a lightly settled region where people exchange local goods.

trawlers: boats that tow large, cone-shaped nets to catch fish.

tributaries: small streams or rivers that feed into larger rivers.

FURTHER INFORMATION

FURTHER INFORMATION

TIME LINE

B.C.

15000–20000	People from Asia are believed to have migrated to North America.
8000–12000	First people are believed to have arrived in the Amazon basin.
3000	Large settlements are established near present-day Manaus, Brazil.
300-1300	At least 100,000 people live on what is now called Marajo Island in the Amazon delta.

A.D.

1500	Vincente Pincon finds the mouth of the Amazon.
1542	Francisco de Orellano travels the length of the Amazon.
1840s	Alfred Wallace provides the first detailed descriptions of the Amazon basin's plants and animals.
1920s	The "rubber boom" ends in the Amazon basin.
1960s	The first Amazon Indian reservations are created by the Villias Boa brothers.
1970-1979	The TransAmazonian highway is built across the Amazon basin in Brazil.
1988	Chico Mendes, rubber tapper and environmentalist, is assassinated.
1992	Brazil hosts the first Earth Summit in Rio de Janeiro.

BOOKS

Castner, James L. *Deep in the Amazon* (series). (Benchmark Books, 2002)

Jermyn, Leslie. *Brazil.* (Gareth Stevens, 1999)

Johnson, Darv. *The Amazon Rain Forest.* (Lucent Books, 1999)

Lewington, Anna. *The Amazonian Indians.* (Peter Bedrick Books, 2001)

Montgomery, Sy. *Encantado: Pink Dolphin of the Amazon.* (Houghton Mifflin, 2002)

Pollard, Michael. *The Amazon.* (Benchmark Books, 1997)

WEB SITES

Amazon River Dolphins
www.virtualeplorers.org/ARD/
Highlights of a trip to study river dolphins in the Amazon basin.

An Amazon Adventure
http://jajhs.kana.k12.wv.us/amazon/index.htm
A variety of information on the Amazon River and the people and wildlife of the river basin.

Discovering the Amazon: The World's Greatest River
www.exploratorium.edu/learning_studio/news/february97.html
An account of a trip down the Amazon River.

Waterworlds
www.pbs.org/journeyintoamazonia/waterworlds.html
Information on the creatures that live in the Amazon River.

Passport to the Rain Forest
www.passporttoknowledge.com/rainforest/main.html
Information about rain forest animals and plants.

Welcome to the Kid's Corner
www.ran.org/kids_action/
A link from the Rain Forest Action Network web site. Facts about the rain forest.

INDEX

INDEX

Numbers in **boldface** type refer to illustrations and maps.